The Subject Tonight Is Love

60 Wild and Sweet Poems of

Hafiz

Versions by Daniel James Ladinsky
Pumpkin House Press

International Standard Book Number: 0-9657637-0-6
Library of Congress Catalog Card: 96-92272
First Edition 1996
Second Edition 1997

This book is available through the Pumpkin House Press for $12.00 a copy. Postage, handling and taxes are included in that price; we offer normal discounts to bookstores on orders of five or more copies. One may write Post Office Box 1625, North Myrtle Beach, South Carolina 29598, U.S.A.; Fax: (803) 272-3228; or e-mail: PumpkinH@aol.com.

"The Subject Tonight Is Love" was printed by Sheriar Press with the encouragement and contributions of Andy Lesnik, Sheila Krynski and Ann Conlon. Sheriar Press and Sheriar Foundation are the publishers and distributors of many high quality esoteric books, specializing particularly in books by or about Meher Baba. A catalogue is available upon written request from Sheriar Press, 3005 Highway 17 North Bypass, Myrtle Beach, South Carolina 29577, U.S.A.

The cover is based upon a page of the Gulistan (Rose Garden) by the 13th century poet Saadi. Although the original painting is not signed, it has been attributed to Payag, the brother of the famous Mughal painter Balchand. My sincere thanks to the owners of this painting.

The words in Persian script on the cover are from a Saadi poem.

Contents

Acknowledgments

This book has come into being from the efforts and love of many, and it is with gratitude and pleasure that I list the following names.

My thanks to Kathleen Barker who has devoted hundreds of hours to this work. She has helped design the cover and the text, she has typeset everything, she has helped me polish these poems with her music and love, and has given of herself remarkably. I think she is a real angel who is trying to live amongst us in this strange world.

Eric Nadel, Mark Riney, John Talmo, Dennis McCabe, Marshall Hay, Max Reif, Frank & Elaine McNutt, Big Nick, Emily Meyer, Ben Hay, Gabe and Flint Mednick, Ellen Book, Carole Kelly, Sylvia Cheek, Jeff Wolverton, Glen and Laurel, Beth and Chris, Jim Wrobel, and Hermes have all been helpful.

A special thanks to Jim Meyer who has contributed to this work and has put several of my Hafiz poems to some splendid music. And my thanks to Mary Lloyd Dugan who has made a children's book from one of the Hafiz poems called "Dance In The Breeze." I also want to thank Mary Lloyd for some very fine music with which she has dressed some of the poems.

A big thanks to Hettie Johnson for proofreading this manuscript and for feeding me at times. And a special thanks to Andy Lesnik who sweetly volunteered his mega-buck-an-hour honed Harvard brain to do most of the final proofreading. Any errors you may catch is because this work keeps evolving. I wake each day to find new lush growth in this fertile summer field of poems and text. And I go after all that divine green – intoxicated with excitement – swinging my farmer's hoe against the Macintosh keys and putting dashes and commas – and inventing unique punctuation – just Everywhere@#*^+=^ as I may be doing^@^ right now! Help! Someone tie me up and carry off this book to the market place before I ruin this bumper crop that Hafiz so graciously sowed.

My thanks to Steve Klein who is a royal man and was a great help with some hundred Hafiz poems a while back and just recently did some more proofreading; thanks to Duck (who is a royal woman) and to Josh (a prince). And my thanks to dear Nancy Wall – who deserves lavish praise.

A special thanks to Hank Mindlin, who was the editor and the principal collaborator on another volume of Hafiz poetry that strikes me as remarkable, a book called "I Heard God Laughing." And a very special thanks to the many people that worked with Hank that I have yet to meet. And thanks to Mischa Rutenberg, and again to Hank – for their great music and a wonderful time I had performing with them. Thanks to dear Paula Gordon, who ran up a big phone and fax bill because of her love for this project, and who has made some very timely suggestions to the work. A big hug and thanks to Karen Kaye too.

Nancy Barton has made a valued contribution to this book, as has Maria Radoje, a talented young musician visiting from England, an excellent cellist and composer who, by the way, is looking for a good job in the U.S.A.

I want to thank Roslyn Taubman for the beauty and extraordinary support she brought to this work in its very earliest stages. And I want to credit her with the clever name of Pumpkin House Press – that will mean something only to those who know of Meher Baba's life.

And a double big thanks to an old friend, Nancy Wurzel, who came through for Hafiz, taking time from her busy professorship in Ohio, and a new litter of wonderful cats, to read through this one last go. You are loved.

And my thanks to Mani S. Irani, Dr. Goher, Aloba, Bal Natu, Meherwan Jessawala and Manu, Bhau Kalchuri, Katie's wonderful wrath, and to my dear departed friend Pendu, and to everyone in my Meherazad and Meherabad family.

Thanks to the beautiful Meher Spiritual Center and all its devoted workers. Thanks to the Sunday night poetry meeting.

And my very deepest thanks to a man named Eruch, who has given so much love to so many.

Introduction

My work with Hafiz began on an early morning walk in the countryside of India, on a beautiful tree lined road that leads to a place I hope you may someday visit called Meherazad.

I was walking with an elderly Zoroastrian man who lived for most of his life with Meher Baba and was one of His most dear and closest disciples, until Meher Baba's passing in 1969. We were talking about Hafiz, who was Baba's favorite poet. And I was somewhat raving about how sad it seemed to me that the Western world knew so little of that Great Old One's (Hafiz's) astounding love and spirit. Thus began this work. That night, working from a literal translation, I wrote my first version of a Hafiz poem.

All the poems here are based on that remarkable translation of the "Divan of Hafiz," by H. Wilberforce Clarke, originally published in 1891. I work from a beautiful two volume, 1011 page edition of Clarke's work recently republished in Iran. I also borrow and shape ideas and thoughts from several thousand other pages of material and poems that are attributed to Hafiz and his life.

The number of poems that are said to have been "written" by Hafiz varies; according to Clarke there are 693.

I believe there is a profoundly greater love, light and treasure in the eyes of Hafiz than is available in all the portraits (i.e., books and poems) of him that I have seen. Because of this belief I have expounded on the poems in his "Divan." From what I feel to be the heart or the spirit of a particular poem (or poems), I have often written many interpretations. Thus my work with Hafiz is clearly a version, as defined: "A description or account from one point of view."

It is my understanding that Hafiz never actually wrote poetry, but only spoke it out loud or sang it when in the mood. And some of the most respected scholars feel that the first complete manuscript of his poems wasn't even compiled until many years after his passing. Still I feel there is a tremendous foundation that has been provided from which one can render a living portrait of Hafiz.

I have been told by those who know the nuances of the language that Hafiz, when read in Persian, can appear extraordinarily rich, robust and alive, even Perfect, to one who understands him. Although I do not speak the Persian language, and have given up my study of it, I listen to hours of Hafiz's poetry being recited and sung in his vernacular in order to get some idea of how sound in itself can become a tangible and nurturing hand. And as I devote myself more to the study of the "Divan of Hafiz" and his life, the more I come to believe that what the Western world sees of him is but a tiny fraction, such a tiny fraction, of one of history's most magnificent teachers and friends.

Most of what I see of Hafiz's verse, caged in the restrictive English language, saddens me. For the verses usually appear as golden bones – sometimes stripped so bare of Reality and Music that some miracle of DNA reconstruction seems to be needed to restore the holy sinew and hair, guts and grandeur, so that Hafiz might be himself again and dance, roar and laugh, while helping us to play catch with the Sun; "O, play catch with the Sun!"

Words like "translation" or "version" in regard to the Divine (as I view Hafiz's abode) are meaningless and absurd unless they can communicate light and humor and give us comfort; unless they can let us sit with the Beloved for a moment; unless they give access to hope and can spill a flammable insight all over us and then – even strike a welcomed match.

The simple but profound gauge of judging Truth's presence in any words attributed to Hafiz should always be: Does God live close enough to them to kick you with His beautiful foot? Do they have the grace, power and the majesty to bestow that degree of love that can aid our divine Transformation?

I have written some 4,500 renderings since I began my study of the "Divan" and Hafiz in the Fall of 1992. These are among the first to be published. Most are not complete. For the majority of the poems still appear to me as uncut diamonds, and I know if I give them further care and love, they will reveal a greater brilliance and more of their tender and playful facets of God.

In another volume of Hafiz poetry that has been recently published (called "I Heard God Laughing"), there is a rendering of some of my favorite lines of Hafiz. These lines to me reveal so much of him. Upon being asked what is a poet Hafiz responds: "A poet is someone who can pour light into a cup, then raise it to nourish your beautiful parched, holy mouth." May some of these poems give you that wondrous taste – give you a few moments of respite in the arms of the Sweet Reality.

Sometimes I feel that I have just begun to open a sacred music box that Hafiz wound up. Just the other day I caught him in the "Tavern" singing:

"No one could ever paint a Too Wonderful picture of my heart or God."

Sometimes I feel that I have just begun to wade – with my little cane pole and piece of string with a hook on it – between the lines in the "Divan" where Hafiz seems to have stocked deep pools with beautiful shining fish that want to leap out into our world and give us nourishment and love and rides upon their backs.

I hope to continue throughout my life the study of Hafiz, who has been known for centuries as "The Tongue Of The Invisible." I hope to go through his "Divan" again and again, and to be able to write with a greater strength, depth and purity. I have prayed hundreds of times like a sweet madman for help with this work and for the ability to make known and clear a few notes of the Luminous Sound Of God, which I feel I once literally heard and saw in Hafiz, when he, as a Resplendent Fountaining Sun, sang hundreds of lines to me in a remarkable Dream.

I treat this work with the utmost respect and care. I am in gratitude for having completed what I have thus far.

What can I say to my dear Master, Meher Baba, for all His help and guidance. For whatever truth, beauty, laughter and charm you may find here, I would say, it is a gift to this world from Him, the Avatar.

Daniel Ladinsky
April 7, 1997

Know

The true nature of your Beloved.

In His loving eyes your every thought,

Word and movement is always –

Always Beautiful.

Hafiz

Comments About Hafiz And Existing Works

Shams-ud-din Muhammad Hafiz was born in Shiraz, Persia. The dates attributed to his birth and death vary; they are commonly believed to be 1320 to 1389.

I feel that most readers who pick up this book will have some knowledge of Hafiz, so rather than go into a long sketch of his life, I would just like to reflect upon some of the more important translations of which I am aware and to make a few more comments about my own work, and rather presumptuously attempt to "define" Hafiz.

In Gertrude Bell's "Teachings of Hafiz," The Octagon Press, London, 186 pages, a reprint of her original 1897 work, there are some hundred pages of preface, introduction and notes on the life, times and poems of Hafiz. Her translations of Hafiz, though few in number, are considered some of the best of that century.

In the H. Wilberforce Clarke work there are 40 pages of introduction to the life of Hafiz and a literary history and outline of the sources Clarke used.

Probably the most accessible book of Hafiz's poetry found in the U.S.A. today is "Fifty Poems of Hafiz" by A. J. Arberry (recently reprinted by Curzon Press). It contains an excellent 34 page introduction. And just recently I came across the Hafiz book entitled "The Green Sea of Heaven," translated by Elizabeth T. Gray, published by the White Cloud Press, 1995, which strikes me as a wonderful and important brush stroke toward portraying and revealing the majesty of "God's Tongue" – Hafiz.

The contemporary Australian writer, Paul Smith, has written a version of the "Divan of Hafiz," 791 poems, New Humanity Press, Melbourne. In a separate 256 page book, Mr. Smith has put together probably the greatest collection of literary facts and history concerning Hafiz in the English language. This book also includes what Smith feels is the life story of Hafiz.

Included in Smith's work are some intriguing quotes about Hafiz and his poetry by such personalities as Emerson, Goethe, the famous Sufi teacher Inayat Khan, and Edward Fitzgerald, best known for his version of the Rubaiyat of Omar Khayyam.

What I say on the back cover of this book basically summarizes the life of Hafiz in my view. And the profundity of that statement reveals his unique role and significance – allowing the reader of his poetry not only to see and taste for a moment something of our True Self, but to begin to grow and unfold from the essential nutrients therein.

Who is Hafiz? He is our very Destiny. He is someone who reached that stage, or station, in his evolutionary/involutionary process and thus naturally fell crazy in love with God. But, he was also someone with whom God fell in love, with whom God married, as it were, making Hafiz's verse sanctified, making Hafiz's verse God's own Divine Offspring.

Hafiz is considered one of the greatest lyrical poets of all time. I lack a musical background, but have tried to maintain his lyrical quality as best I can. Hundreds of times I could have easily rhymed lines but chose not to, feeling that to do so might have diluted the image I was trying to bring out and enhance. Instead, I have concentrated in this work mostly on excavating, laying bare and unveiling the astonishing charm and substance that I find ingrained within the "Divan."

As Hafiz's poems are inherently ecstatic and sacred, they are all firmly rooted in the Mystical Ground of Unreason – and a love and experience that surpasses the intellect, time and space. Thus it seems so very natural often to depart from any scholarly disciplines that might leave Hafiz looking pale, small, dated, or in any way lacking – as I know him to be so very much to the contrary. A tiny example of departing from what I consider to be the "finite or republican approach to Hafiz" is the occasional developed refrain in some of the poems that to my mind seems realistic, innate, and much closer to the Spirit of the verse. A larger example is the several thousand renderings of Hafiz that I have done hoping to convey something of his vital connection to the heart of every lover of God, and his vital connection to our Age, to the present day, and to the advents of the Beloved.

I love the texture of truth and image Hafiz expresses in one of his poems, contained in this book, when he says:

"I have been lifted drunk off the floor in a Magnificent Tavern.
Now at my seat upon Divine Love

I gaze at Everything with brilliant clear eyes –
I can so easily lean my cheek across the small table of time and space
And let you touch my beautiful, laughing, wooly beard."

In translating Hafiz, or doing renderings, one has the awesome task – if one is to be considered successful – of bringing to the reader's senses the Splendid Knowledge, the gifts of courage, humor and intimacy with the Sun. As Hafiz says himself, "Having the strength to turn the Divine Pockets of the Hidden inside out." For indeed a wondrous, charming, gifted, Sweet Drunk Man and Light – a wild holy friend to the world – is how Hafiz would appear if we could somehow get sound equipment and film into the past.

I feel this wonderful 14th century poet had a special love for and interest in artists. For the true artist and the mystic meet over the same cup and have that precious talent to impart its contents of Truth and freedom. I hope that someday many of his verses can again be put into songs, paintings and performances, as music and dance was often the medium, the very catalyst for their original spontaneous expression.

Persian poets of Hafiz's era would often address themselves in the poems as if carrying on a conversation. This was considered a method of "signing" the poem as one might a painting or a letter to a friend. I have not eliminated this characteristic that sometimes makes the verse seem more intimate, playful and real. The reader should also note that sometimes Hafiz speaks from the point of view of a seeker, other times from the point of view of a realized Master and Guide. It is believed that after living with his Murshid for some 40 years Hafiz received the Divine Mantle of God Realization, and that during his early life with his Teacher, Hafiz had composed, sung, many of the poems that are now attributed to him.

Ralph Waldo Emerson said,

"Hafiz defies you to show him or put him in a condition inopportune or ignoble...He fears nothing. He sees too far; he sees throughout; such is the only man I wish to...be."

I just returned from two months in India a few days ago as I write (first printing). I would say I have the great fortune of having a spiritual friend and teacher, an elderly man whom I have known for nearly twenty years and whom I have been able to live close to at times – eat beside, walk beside, hear him belch and laugh, and even catch the flu from him this last trip; and also feel my head get severed and roll in excruciating pain when my foolishness surged too much. As with any true teacher, I feel he wants nothing from anyone, but only wants you to know the priceless treasure of serving, loving and becoming consciously closer to God. And speaking of all the greatness of Hafiz on these last few pages reminds me of something I was able to read to my friend as we one day walked in the early morning on that "beautiful tree lined road." What I read was this:

> "The Perfect Ones such as Rumi, Hafiz, Kabir and Saadi – as moving and sublime as their words and effect can be – are sometimes not clearly understood. That is, as magnificent and vital as are their roles in creation they are just shadows of the Avatar, the Christ, the Prophet. The glorious Perfect Ones whirl in the Beloved's Tavern Window – they all sing to the world saying, 'Come drink from the Heart of the Friend. Come let your every cell and the eye of your soul know the Resplendent Nourishment and Compassion, the Divine Beauty and Grace of the ever present Ancient One.'"

"Come drink from the heart of the Friend." Throughout this book the words Friend and Beloved are mentioned many times. These words, as also the words Ocean, Sky, Sun and Moon when capitalized in these poems, can be a direct reference, a synonym, for the word God.

As one might have endearing pet names for family members or friends – Hafiz has a unique vocabulary of names for God. God to him is more than just the Father, the Mother, the Infinite or a Being beyond comprehension. Hafiz calls God a range of names, some are: the Sweet Uncle, the Generous Merchant, the Immediate One, the Problem Giver, the Problem Solver, the Clever Rascal. To him, God is someone we can meet, enter, and begin to eternally explore. God is the Dancer, the Music, the Wine, the Bottle, the Beautiful Companion, the Kind Radiant One. In these poems Hafiz gives the address of the holes in the roof, the cracks in the walls, and to the front and back doors of God's favorite Taverns – so that our mouths and souls and lives can stop pretending to be empty or dry.

DJL

Dedicated to
The Saheb-e-Zaman

And to His beautiful companions
Whom I have lived with
And loved.

Where Dolphins Dance

Again
The work starts
As soon as you open your eyes in the
Morning.

Hopefully you got
Some good rest last night.

Why go into the city or the fields
Without first kissing
The Friend

Who always stands at your door?
It takes only a second.

Habits are human nature –
Why not create some that will mint
Gold?

Your arms are violin bows
Always moving.

I have become very conscious upon
Whom we all play.

Thus my eyes have filled with warm
Soft oceans of divine music

Where jeweled dolphins dance
Then leap into this
World.

The Woman I Love

Because the Woman I love lives
Inside of you,

I lean as close to your body with my words
As I can –

And I think of you all the time, dear pilgrim.

Because the One I love goes with you
Wherever you go,
Hafiz will always be near.

If you sat before me, wayfarer,
With your aura bright from your many
Charms,

My lips could resist rushing to you and needing
To befriend your blushed cheek,

But my eyes can no longer hide
The wondrous fact of who
You Really are.

The Beautiful One whom I adore
Has pitched His royal tent inside of you,

So I will always lean my heart
As close to your soul
As I can.

Forgiveness Is The Cash

Forgiveness
Is the cash you need.

All the other kinds of silver really buy
Just strange things.

Everything has its music.
Everything has genes of God inside.

But learn from those courageous addicted lovers
Of glands and opium and gold –

Look,
They cannot jump high or laugh long
When they are whirling.

And the moon and the stars become sad
When their tender light is used for
Night wars.

Forgiveness is part of the treasure you need
To craft your falcon wings
And return

To your true realm of
Divine freedom.

All The Hemispheres

Leave the familiar for a while.
Let your senses and bodies stretch out

Like a welcomed season
Onto the meadows and shores and hills.

Open up to the Roof.
Make a new water-mark on your excitement
And love.

Like a blooming night flower,
Bestow your vital fragrance of happiness
And giving
Upon our intimate assembly.

Change rooms in your mind for a day.

All the hemispheres in existence
Lie beside an equator
In your heart.

Greet Yourself
In your thousand other forms
As you mount the hidden tide and travel
Back home.

All the hemispheres in heaven
Are sitting around a fire
Chatting

While stitching themselves together
Into the Great Circle inside of
You.

The Vegetables

Today
The vegetables would like to be cut

By someone who is singing God's Name.

How could Hafiz know
Such top secret information?

Because
Once we were all tomatoes,

Potatoes, onions or
Zucchini.

At This Party

I don't want to be the only one here
Telling all the secrets –

Filling up all the bowls at this party,
Taking all the laughs.

I would like you
To start putting things on the table
That can also feed the soul
The way I do.

That way
We can invite

A hell of a lot more
Friends.

Why All This Talk

Why all this talk of the Beloved,
Music and dancing,

And
Liquid ruby-light we can lift in a cup?

Because it is low tide,
A very low tide in this age
And around most hearts.

We are exquisite coral reefs,
Dying when exposed to strange
Elements.

God is the wine-ocean we crave –
We miss

Flowing in and out of our
Pores.

In A Handful Of God

Poetry reveals that there is no empty space.

When your truth forsakes its shyness,
When your fears surrender to your strengths,
You will begin to experience

That all existence
Is a teeming sea of infinite life.

In a handful of ocean water
You could not count all the finely tuned
Musicians

Who are acting stoned
For very intelligent and sane reasons

And of course are becoming extremely sweet
And wild.

In a handful of the sky and earth,
In a handful of God,

We cannot count
All the ecstatic lovers who are dancing there
Behind the mysterious veil.

True art reveals there is no void
Or darkness.

There is no loneliness to the clear-eyed mystic
In this luminous, brimming
Playful world.

Because Of Our Wisdom

In many parts of this world water is
Scarce and precious.

People sometimes have to walk
A great distance

Then carry heavy jugs upon their
Heads.

Because of our wisdom, we will travel
Far for love.

All movement is a sign of
Thirst.

Most speaking really says,
"I am hungry to know you."

Every desire of your body is holy;

Every desire of your body is
Holy.

Dear one,
Why wait until you are dying

To discover that divine
Truth?

We Keep Each Other Happy

Like two lovers who have become lost
In a winter blizzard

And find a cozy empty hut
In the forest,

I now huddle everywhere
With the Friend.

God and I have built an immense fire
Together.

We keep each other happy
And warm.

Castrating An Ego

The only problem with not castrating
A gigantic ego is

That it will surely become amorous
And father
A hundred screaming ideas and kids

Who will then all quickly grow up
And skillfully proceed

To run up every imaginable debt
And complication of which your brain
Can conceive.

This would concern normal parents
And any seekers of freedom

And the local merchants nearby
As well.

They could very easily become forced
To disturb your peace;

All those worries and bills could turn to
Wailing ghosts.

The only problem with not lassoing
A runaway ego is

You won't have much desire to sing
In this sweet
World.

This Place Where You Are Right Now

This place where you are right now
God circled on a map for you.

Wherever your eyes and arms and heart can move
Against the earth and sky,
The Beloved has bowed there –

Our Beloved has bowed there knowing
You were coming.

I could tell you a priceless secret about
Your real worth, dear pilgrim,

But any unkindness to yourself,
Any confusion about others,

Will keep one
From accepting the grace, the love,

The sublime freedom
Divine knowledge always offers to you.

Never mind, Hafiz, about
The great requirements this path demands
Of the wayfarers,

For your soul is too full of wine tonight
To withhold the wondrous Truth from this world.

But because I am so clever and generous,
I have already clearly woven a resplendent lock
Of His tresses

As a remarkable truth and gift
In this poem for you.

In A Tree House

Light
Will someday split you open
Even if your life is now a cage,

For a divine seed, the crown of destiny,
Is hidden and sown on an ancient, fertile plain
You hold the title to.

Love will surely bust you wide open
Into an unfettered, blooming new galaxy

Even if your mind is now
A spoiled mule.

A life-giving radiance will come,
The Friend's gratuity will come –

O look again within yourself,
For I know you were once the elegant host
To all the marvels in creation.

From a sacred crevice in your body
A bow rises each night
And shoots your soul into God.

Behold the Beautiful Drunk Singing One
From the lunar vantage point of love.

He is conducting the affairs
Of the whole universe

While throwing wild parties
In a tree house – on a limb
In your heart.

We Are A Couple Of Barroom Sailors

I wake from a nap
And the same clear words greet my mind
That I say every day upon waking,

"Where can I find the Friend?"

I eat and dress and labor
For only one reason.

But why explain about the essential today
And demean the holy?

We are a couple of barroom sailors,
Marooned,

In need of good drink and fine company
To true our perceptions.

Otherwise,
I get a tad concerned about that odd look
That sometimes creeps into your eyes –

That seems to mistake me for a pretty,
Available mermaid.

Upon waking each day
My first words to my heart always are

"Tell me all your news of
Love."

No Other Kind Of Light

Find that flame, that existence,

That Wonderful Man

Who can burn beneath the water.

No other kind of light

Will cook the food you

Need.

Not With Wings

Here soar
Not with wings,

But with your moving hands and feet
And sweating brows –

Standing by your Beloved's side
Reaching out to comfort this world

With your cup of solace
Drawn from your vast reservoir of Truth.

Here soar
Not with your eyes and senses

That turn their backs
On the earth's sweet stumbling dance
Which needs you.

Here love, O here love,
With your mouth tender and open upon your lover,

And with your heart on duty
To the souls of rivers, children, forest animals,
All the shy feathered ones and laughing, jumping,
Shining fish.

O here, pilgrim,
Love
On this holy battleground of life

Where there are bleeding men
Who are calling for a sacred drink,

A gentle word or touch from man
Or God.

Hafiz, why just serve and play with angels?
They are already content.

Brew your knowledge well for men
With aching minds and guts,

And for those wayfarers who have gained
The rare courageous thirsts
That can never be relinquished
Until Union!

Hafiz,
Leave your recipes in golden drums.

Tie those barrels to the backs of camels
Who will keep circumambulating the worlds,

Giving nourishment
To all our tender wondrous spheres.

O here love, O love right here.
Find your happiness, dear wayfarer,

With your beautiful lips and body
So sweetly opened,

Yielding their vital gifts upon
This magnificent
Earth.

Venus Just Asked Me

Perhaps
For just one minute out of the day,

It may be of value to torture yourself
With thoughts like,

"I should be doing
A hell of a lot more with my life than I am –
Cause I'm so damn talented."

But remember,
For just one minute out of the day.

With all the rest of your time,
It would be best
To try
Looking upon your self more as God does.

For He knows
Your true royal nature.

God is never confused
And can see Only Himself in you.

My dear,
Venus just leaned down and asked me
To tell you a secret, to confess

She's just a mirror who has been stealing
Your light and music for centuries.

She knows as does Hafiz,
You are the sole heir to
The King.

The Size Of The Love-Bruise

The

Gauge of a good poem is

The size of the love-bruise it leaves

On your neck.

Or

The size of the love-bruise it can paint

On your brain.

Or

The size of the love-bruise it can weave

Into your soul.

Or indeed –

It could be all of the

Above.

The Theater Of Freedom

In my divine studio
What I have been working on is this:

Painting the Truth,
Revealing
A more realistic picture of God,

Tearing down the cruel walls
That separate you from the tenderness of Fire.

Someone must be withholding
The crucial lines
In all those stories you have heard of our
Friend,

For there is still too much fear
And pallor upon your cheeks,

And I rarely see you
In the marvelous Theater of Freedom.

Hafiz knows
You could not describe him

Even if we sat side by side on a caravan
For years,

Even if we slept close in my desert tent
And you became familiar

With the holy scent
That the sun and my Master leave
Whenever they visit me,

For something has happened
To your youthful passions,

That great fuel
You once had to defend yourself
Against becoming tamed.

And your eyes now often tell me
That your once vital talent to extract joy
From the air
Has fallen into a sleep.

All that you could ever say of me
Can only describe my camel's tail –

And that coarse hair
That is barely visible sometimes
On the left side of the moon's nose.

In my divine studio
Where I am sitting right now
Crafting your heart, lyre
And flute,

I long for the day when you will join me
In knowing

The extraordinary humor
And all the enchanting realities

Of the infinite performances
of
God.

You Say, I Say

You say,
"How can I find God?"

I say,
"The Friend is the lining in your pocket –
The curved pink wall in your belly –

Sober up,
Steady your aim,
Reach in,
Turn the Universe and
The Beautiful Rascal
Inside out."

You say,
"That sounds preposterous –
I really don't believe God is in there."

I say,
"Well then,
Why not try the Himalayas –

You could get naked
And pretend to be an exalted yogi
And eat bark and snow for forty years."

And you might think,

"Hey, Old Man,
Why don't you – go shovel
Snowflakes!"

Where Do You Think You Will Be?

I am sitting on a mountain.
I am casting shadows into the sky.

I did not invite it but the sun has come
And is now playing tag with my feet.

I am whispering to clouds today,
"Watch out for my shoulders,"

For I wish no harm
To all my soft friends.

Where do you think you will Be
When God reveals Himself
Inside of you?

I was so glad to hear
That every pillow in this world
Will become stuffed with
My soul and beard.

I am sitting on a mountain range.
I am a precious body of living water
Offered to the earth
From Light's own hands.

Why ever talk of miracles
When you are destined to become
Infinite love.

Still, the Final Grace was left:
For all of existence and Hafiz to blend
And to find that I am every pillow
Offering comfort

To each mind and
Foot.

The Day Sky

Let us be like
Two falling stars in the day sky.

Let no one know of our sublime beauty
As we hold hands with God
And burn

Into a sacred existence that defies –
That surpasses

Every description of ecstasy
And love.

Among Strong Men

My soul is like a young doe-eyed maid

With lips
Still bruised from last night's divine passion.

But my Master makes me live
Like a humble servant

When any king would trade his throne
For the splendor my eye can see.

Call it many things –
Give your desires polite names
If you must;

Mask the primal instinct from your reality

If you cannot bear that sacred edge
That will hone your ken
Against the Sun and earth.

Among strong men in the Tavern
I can speak a truth

No one will laugh at:
My heart is like a wild alley cat in heat.

In every possible way I conspire
To know freedom and love.

Forget about the common reason, Hafiz,
For it only enslaves.

There is something holy deep inside of you
That is so ardent and awake,

That needs to lie down naked
Next to God.

Beautiful Hands

This is the kind of Friend
You are –

Without making me realize

My soul's anguished history,

You slip into my house at night,

And while I am sleeping,

You silently carry off

All my suffering and sordid past

In Your beautiful
Hands.

Old Sweet Beggar

This
Path to God
Made me such an old sweet beggar.

I was starving until one night
My love tricked God Himself
To fall into my bowl.

Now Hafiz is infinitely rich,
But all I ever want to do

Is keep emptying out
My emerald-filled
Pockets

Upon
This tear-stained
World.

Out Of The Mouths Of A Thousand Birds

Listen –
Listen more carefully to what is around you
Right now.

In my world
There are the bells from the clanks
Of the morning milk drums,

And a wagon wheel outside my window
Just hit a bump

Which turned into an ecstatic chorus
Of the Beloved's Name.

There is the Prayer Call
Rising up like the sun
Out of the mouths of a thousand birds.

There is an astonishing vastness
Of movement and Life

Emanating sound and light
From my folded hands

And my even quieter simple being and heart.

My dear,
Is it true that your mind
Is sometimes like a battering
Ram

Running all through the city,
Shouting so madly inside and out

About the ten thousand things
That do not matter?

Hafiz, too,
For many years beat his head in youth

And thought himself at a great distance,
Far from an armistice
With God.

But that is why this scarred old pilgrim
Has now become such a sweet rare vintage
Who weeps and sings for you.

That is why Hafiz will forever in his verse
Play his cymbal and call to you.

O listen –
Listen more carefully
To what is inside of you right now.

In my world
All that remains is the wondrous call to
Dance and prayer

Rising up like a thousand suns
Out of the mouth of a
Single bird.

I Knew We Would Be Friends

As soon as you opened your mouth
And I heard your soft
Sounds,

I knew we would be
Friends.

The first time, dear pilgrim, I heard
You laugh,

I knew it would not take me long
To turn you back into
God.

Build A House For Men

You have taken root in the Beloved.
I love your golden branches

And the hundred graceful movements
Your body now makes each time
The wind, children and love
Come near.

Build a house for men and birds.
Sit with them – play music.

For a day, for just one day,
Talk about that which disturbs no one
And bring some peace into your
Beautiful eyes.

Why play notes from your soft mouth-flute
That hurt the Blue Sky's ear?

The Friend has such exquisite taste
That every time you bow to Him

Your mind will become lighter and more
Refined;
Your spirit will prepare its voice to laugh
In an outrageous freedom.

You have taken root in our Beloved.
I love your emerald branches
And the hundred ways your heart does dance

Every time you discover God is so pleased
Because His hands are always playing catch
With your soul!

That Sounds Wonderful

Good poetry
Makes a beautiful naked woman
Materialize from
Words,

Who then says,
With a sword precariously waving
In her hands,

"If you look at my loins
I will cut off your head,

And reach down and grab your spirit
By its private parts,

And carry you off to heaven
Squealing in joy."

Hafiz says,
"That sounds wonderful, just
Wonderful.

Someone please – start writing
Some great
Lines."

A Singing Cleaning Woman

A leaf says,

"Sweethearts – don't pick me,
For I am busy doing
God's work.

I am lowering my veins and roots
Like ropes

With buckets tied to them
Into the earth's deep
Lake.

I am drawing water
That I offer like a rose to
The sky.

I am a singing cleaning woman
Dusting all the shelves in
The air

With my elegant green
Rags.

I have a heart.
I can know happiness like
You."

Your Shape Of Laughter

Let my words become like a skilled
Potter's hands,

Quieting,
Smoothing your life
With their knowledge,

Reaching into your tender core
And spreading you out
Like the morning

That leaps from the sun's amused wink
Onto hills, brows and the backs of so many
Beautiful laboring beasts.

God's duty is to make perfect
All your movements of mind, of limb,
And your ascending shape of laughter.

Watch the way my hands dance
With their diamond-edged brilliance

Cutting you open with music,
Reaching into your heart

And spilling the night sky-jar you carry
That is always full of giggling planets and stars.

My words are a divine potter's wheel.
If you stay near to me,
Please,
Stay near to me –

And Hafiz will spin you into
Love.

Something I Have Learned

Water
Gets poured through a cloth
To become free of impurities.

The Beloved's Name
Is a mystical weave and pattern –

A hidden sieve of effulgence
We need to pass through thousands of
Times.

From my constant remembrance
Of the Friend,

All I now say is safe to
Drink.

Something that I have learned
From the Kind Radiant One

Who drew me from the unfathomable
Sky's well

Makes me playful all day
Long.

And A Big Herd Of Sweet Goats

I used to walk in a beautiful garden
Singing,

But the garden fell in love with my
Voice,
And fell in love with my toes too,

Then concluded it would be smart
To just follow me home
And never move!

The same thing happened with the sun,
Then Saturn and a dozen other
Vacationing, inebriated
Planets –

And a whole near-by mountain range
With their trees and streams and fish still tied
Onto their backs –

And a big herd of sweet, lively goats.

My dear, what Hafiz is really trying to say is:
If you ever get
Lonely,

Come visit this Wild house –
My Celestial Verse –

Where all of us will always
So happily live.

Narrow The Difference

When I play my lute,
The invisible ones call a conference,

And the angels travel far knowing
A rare entertainment will soon take place.

When I play my drum, my notes become so real
The winged ones throw saddles upon them;
An outrageous holy rodeo begins.

No one has ever sat with Hafiz
And not left for the better.

No one can read my poems out loud
In a tender, loving voice
And not narrow the difference,
Not narrow the gap,
Between you and God.

I have many younger brothers and sisters
Scattered upon this earth.

There are always friends of God in this world.
Find one and offer service.
For their glance is generous and cannot help
But forever give.

When Hafiz plays his lute,
My notes ascend into the air and form
Infinite blue crystals

That will move on the wind's breath for hundreds of years
As my sacred debris, as the divine dust
Rising as a gift from my
Singing bones.

The Small Table Of Time And Space

I am a Golden Compass –
Watch me whirl.

To the east and to the west
To the north and to the south,
In all directions I will true your course
Toward laughter and unity.

To everywhere I will deliver enlightenment
On the backs of camels, birds
And strong pilgrims.

Into every country
I will carry the Holy Names and dance
And dance.

I am a Golden Compass –
Watch me sing and spin
Illustrious strands of lyrics and truth.

I am a divine Agent.
Your passage to light, your ticket,
May need my stamp.

My feet and verse are now ecstatic
And mid-air;
Just place your self beneath our leaping arch –
We will sweetly rain upon you.

Watch me whirl into nothingness
Your fears and darkness –
Just keep tossing them onto my golden plate.

I am a Holy Instrument always tuned by God.
I live beyond every dimension.

I have been lifted drunk off the floor
In a Magnificent Tavern.

Now at my seat upon Divine Love
I gaze at Everything with brilliant, clear eyes.

I can so easily lean my cheek across this small table
Of time and space

And let you touch my beautiful laughing
Wooly beard.

Hafiz is an Emerald Compass.
My knowledge will put manna in your purse.

My only duty that now remains
To this world

Is from every direction
To forever serve you wine and
Hope.

Hafiz is a Golden Skirt
The Beloved has lifted off a magnificent floor
And has tied around His waist.

Watch us whirl, whirl,
Whirl!

The Happy Virus

I caught the happy virus last night

When I was out singing beneath the stars.

It is remarkably contagious –

So kiss me.

The Wonderful Lawlessness

Late in winter
My heart is still a rose in bloom.

Late in summer
I still have snow-covered peaks upon my back
Where we can all play and slide.

At night I need no candle or lamp,
For my soul has forever awakened

To there being just the reality
Of Light
And the wonderful Lawlessness of God.

Late in winter I need no heat,
For I have entered the Infinite Fire.

Come,
Build a sled,
Find a grand hill within my verse –

You and I and God
Should play there more often
Upon a peak such as Hafiz

That the Beloved has carved
So well.

They Call To You To Sing

Stones are longing for what you know.

If they had the graceful movements
Of your feet and tongue,

They would not stop laughing
Between their ecstatic dance steps and unbroken praise.

Your heart beats inside a sacred drum,
Its skin is tanned and stretched –
Our skin is alive and stretched –
With the wild molecules of His Wondrous Existence.

Your mind and eyes are an immense silk cloth
Upon which all your thoughts and movements paint.

Your soul once sat on an easel on my knee.
For ages I have been sketching you
With myriad shapes of sounds and light;

Now awake, dear pilgrim,
With your thousand swaying arms
That need to caress the Sky.

Now awake with your love for the Friend and Creation,
Help this Old Tavern Sweeper, Hafiz,
To celebrate.

No more enemies from this golden view –
All who have entered this holy mountain cave
Have dropped their shields and swords.

We all cook together around a fire
Our yearning music builds.

We share our tools and instruments and plates;
We are companions on this earth

As the sun and planets are in the sky.
We are all sentries at our sacred humble posts.

The stones and stars envy the movements
Of your legs and tongue
And call to you to sing on their behalf.

The atoms in your cells and limbs are full of wonderful talents;
They dance in the Hidden Choir I conduct.

Don't sleep tonight, dear pilgrim,
So I can lead you on my white mare to His Summer House.

This love you now have of the Truth
Will never forsake you.

Your joys and sufferings on this arduous path
Are lifting your worn veil like a rising stage curtain

And will surely reveal your Magnificent Self
So that you can guide this world like Hafiz

In the Hidden Choir
God and His friends will forever
Conduct.

Your Medicine

If you have not

Been taking your medicine lately

By saying your prayers every day,

How can Hafiz seriously listen

To all your heartaches

About life

or

God?

It Happens All The Time In Heaven

It happens all the time in heaven,
And some day

It will begin to happen
Again on earth –

That men and women who are married,
And men and men who are
Lovers,

And women and women
Who give each other
Light,

Often will get down on their knees

And while so tenderly
Holding their lover's hand,

With tears in their eyes,
Will sincerely speak, saying,

"My dear,
How can I be more loving to you;

How can I be more
Kind?"

The Guardians Of His Beauty

We are the guardians of His Beauty.

We are the protectors
Of the Sun.

There is only one reason
We have followed God into this world:

To encourage laughter, freedom, dance
And love.

Let a noble cry inside of you speak to me
Saying,

"Hafiz,
Don't just sit there on the moon tonight
Doing nothing –

Help unfurl my heart into the Friend's Mind,
Help, Old Man, to heal my wounded wings!"

We are the companions of His Beauty.
We are the guardians
Of Truth.

Every man, plant and creature in Existence,
Every woman, child, vein and note
Is a servant of our Beloved –

A harbinger of joy,
The harbinger of
Light.

The Subject Tonight Is Love

The subject tonight is Love

And for tomorrow night as well.

As a matter of fact,

I know of no better topic

For us to discuss

Until we all

Die!

I Saw You Dancing

I saw you dancing last night on the roof
Of your house all alone.

I felt your heart longing for the
Friend.

I saw you whirling
Beneath the soft bright rose
That hung from an invisible stem in
The sky,

So I began to change into my best clothes
In hopes of joining you

Even though
I live a thousand miles away.

And if
You had spun like an immaculate sphere
Just two more times,

Then bowed again so sweetly to
The east,

You would have found God and me
Standing so near
And lifting you into our
Arms.

I saw you dancing last night near the roof
Of this world.

Hafiz feels your soul in mine
Calling for our
Beloved.

Never Say It Is Not Me

I taste what you taste.
I know the kind of lyrics that you most like.

I know which sounds will become resplendent
In your mind
And bring such pleasure to your feet
That they need to jump or whirl.

When anything touches or enters your body
Never say it is not Me,
For God is just trying to get close.

I have no use for divine patience –
My lips are now burning and everywhere.
I am running from every corner of this earth and sky
Wanting to kiss you.

I am every particle of wheat and dust –
I am ground from His Own Body.
I am rioting at your soul's door.
I am spinning in midair like golden, falling leaves
Trying to win your glance.

I am sweetly rolling against your walls and shores all night
Even though you are asleep.
I am singing from the mouth of animals and birds
Honoring God's ancient promise –
His need to let you know the Truth.

My dear,
When anything ever touches or enters your body
Never say it is not Me – for God is just trying,
For the Beloved is just trying, to get close.

Hafiz has fallen into His glass
And is now rushing to your side from every corner
Of existence, needing to say,
"I Am yours."

Absolutely Clear

Don't surrender your loneliness
So quickly.
Let it cut more deep.

Let it ferment and season you
As few human
Or even divine ingredients can.

Something missing in my heart tonight
Has made my eyes so soft,
My voice
So tender,

My need of God
Absolutely
Clear.

Ten Thousand Idiots

It is always a danger
To aspirants
On the
Path

When they begin
To believe and
Act

As if the ten thousand idiots
Who so long ruled
And lived
Inside

Have all packed their bags
And skipped town
Or
Died.

To Anything That Moved

Yesterday it was sweet madness,
Reciting poems for hours

And talking about love to anything that
Moved.

I lay down late thinking I might be able to sleep
All the way until there was the light
Of resplendent sounds – and polished jokes –
From the morning birds.

That was foolish of me,
For in just a few minutes, three worlds
Crawled from a cave in my heart,
Built a huge fire and yelled,
"Get Up!"

They could not contain their happiness
Living inside of one as ripe as I.

We began jumping up and down
And banging our heads
Like a drunk bronze clapper in a sacred Buddhist bell –

Against the fields and mountains,
Against all the jeweled walls of this Universe.

Yesterday was such exquisite madness,
Singing about the Friend for hours

And talking about love to anything
That dared to move.

Yet I believe another wonderful day,
And perhaps even a sweeter height of rare, inspired insanity,
O Hafiz, has just begun.

Carrying God

No one can keep us from carrying God
Wherever we go.

No one can rob His Name
From our hearts as we try to relinquish our fears
And at last stand – Victorious.

We do not have to leave Him in the mosque
Or church alone at night;

We do not have to be jealous of tales of saints
Or glorious masts, those intoxicated souls
Who can make outrageous love with the Friend.

We do not have to be envious of our spirits' ability
Which can sometimes touch God in a dream.

Our yearning eyes, our warm-needing bodies,
Can all be drenched in contentment
And Light.

No one anywhere can keep us
From carrying the Beloved wherever we go.

No one can rob His precious Name
From the rhythm of my heart –
Steps and breath.

I Cherish Your Ears

Dear pilgrim,
I love your shoes, your coat,
Your pants, your hat, your furry head,

Your cup, your bowl,
Your messy closets,

And most of all – I cherish your cute ears.

Why? Don't ask!

Just speak what you love about me.

Come closer if you are feeling
A little timid today
Or dense

Because surely you would find something
Very endearing about
Hafiz.

Then
We can pass many years
Talking so silly,

Like two highly advanced aspirants –
Like two emancipated holy vagrants
Who are sharing His Bottle
Of Truth

And feeling so damn good
And Drunk and Free.

Deepening The Wonder

Death is a favor to us,
But our scales have lost their balance.

The impermanence of the body
Should give us great clarity,
Deepening the wonder in our senses and eyes

Of this mysterious existence we share
And are surely just traveling through.

If I were in the Tavern tonight,
Hafiz would call for drinks

And as the Master poured, I would be reminded
That all I know of life and myself is that

We are just a midair flight of golden wine
Between His Pitcher and His Cup.

If I were in the Tavern tonight,
I would buy freely for everyone in this world

Because our marriage with the Cruel Beauty
Of time and space cannot endure very long.

Death is a favor to us,
But our minds have lost their balance.

The miraculous existence and impermanence of
Form
Always makes the illumined ones
Laugh and sing.

Will Beat You Up

Jealousy
And most all of your sufferings

Are from believing
You know better than God.

Of course,
Such a special brand of arrogance as that
Always proves disastrous,

And will rip the seams
In your caravan tent,

Then cordially invite in many species
Of mean biting flies and
Strange thoughts –

That will
Beat you
Up.

I Follow Barefoot

I long for You so much
I follow barefoot Your frozen tracks

That are high in the mountains
That I know are years old.

I long for You so much
I have even begun to travel
Where I have never been before.

Hafiz, there is no one in this world
Who is not looking for God.

Everyone is trudging along
With as much dignity, courage
And style

As they possibly
Can.

Join Me In The Pure Atmosphere

I slip in and out of the Sea at night with this
Amazed soul I have.

I am like a magnificent, magic ocean turtle
Who sets aside his vast wings of
Blue effulgence

When I crawl upon your shores
To leave my divine seed of verse.

Let me remain cryptic tonight
All the way till dawn
As I orbit God
In this holy, ecstatic mood.

Grab hold of the corners
Of my luminous, tender shell
And I will whirl for you,

For I am covered with eminent crystals
That I have gathered from the infinite depths
Of love.

Follow my tracks in the sand that lead
Beyond thought and space,

For I can see deep down
That you are really a golden bird
That needs to
Dance

With your spirit enraptured and ascending
On the currents of Light—

On the currents of His
Breath.

Join me with your hands, wings, hoofs or fins
In my sublime applause.

Join me in the pure atmosphere of gratitude
For life.

I slip in and out of the Moon each night
With a gracious ease
With this brilliant heart I have.

The Beautiful Friend, the Exquisite One,
Sometimes steps from His Invisible Body
And walks upon our shore

So that we might see and know
His Radiant Tender Shell –

His eminent crowns
That are the three worlds.

O grab hold of the hem of His skirt
As He spins this Universe on an emerald
Dance floor!

Cling to the Transcendent Elements in His glance
As the Beloved forever whirls
His Love.

Hafiz
Slips in and out of God at night
Tied to his own amazed
Soul.

Some Angels Grumble

Every time a man upon the path
Does not keep his
Word,

Some angels grumble
And have to remove a few of
The bets

They had placed upon
His heart
To win.

Playing In The Brilliance

The Pir (the saint) looks out from his boat,
That has sunk
To the bottom of the Ocean.

And he so clearly sees
That all the fish
Are playing in the Soft Brilliance.

The Pir lifts his lute
From the bow of his boat

Then starts singing:

"Dear ones,
Why let your winsome body act
As if it is living against a tyrant's knife?

Why pretend your expansive existence,
Your Imperial Nature,

Have all been squeezed
Into a tiny red hot skillet

That is being kicked by a camel's hoof
Over the dry sand?"

For your friend Hafiz
So clearly sees we are all immersed
In the Soft Brilliance.

We are all just waiting to break camp –
Into God.

Like The Ganges

The Sun needs a sacred tablet where it can write
Its resplendent verse

And Hafiz has become a blessed stone.

When the Friend begins to sway from being so full
Of wine,

Music flows like the Ganges from His mouth.

He then needs fertile banks and walls in this world
To govern all that raging Light.

I build canals into the cities and the plains.
I run beside small villages and sing.

I nourish and cool the roots of stars and trees
And man.

Women wash their clothes in Me.
Thirsty cattle and skinny dogs come

Accompanied by spell-bound children,
But soon we all begin to splash and kiss.

Birds fly to my shores, then get excited and spread
The news:

The verse of Hafiz is a Turkish bath;
The glance of Hafiz is a beatific ocean
Bath

Where all can clean their bodies
In the sounds from my flute and mirth –

In the tenderness of my drum's alluring beat.

His Music has filled my pores.
I am inebriated with the unbearable Truth.

Tonight I am a staggering, awesome planet,
For all day long I construct alliances

Using my divine gravity upon all sinew,
Minds and souls.

I ecstatically speak with words and also with
The purest language – Silence –

Saying in a thousand different ways:

"Dear countrymen, and all my nearby cousins –
Comets and galaxies,

Every amoeba, creature and plant –
Bring your cup and I will pour you God."

O, when the Friend begins to sway
From being so full of love,

Music flows like the Ganges from
My mouth.

And Acting So Cool

The whole world just got thick
Again with
God.

And everywhere I look
Makes me feel very proud

That all the objects and creatures
Can remain looking
So poised

And acting so cool
While keeping the Great Secret
So well

And not blissfully shout
All day long the Reality

I Am –
I Am the Wine!

The whole universe just got stoned
Out of its mind again
On the Beauty
Of God.

A Potted Plant

I pull a sun from my coin purse each day.

And at night I let my pet the moon
Run freely into the sky meadow.

If I whistled,
She would turn her head and look at me.

If I then waved my arms,
She would come back wagging a marvelous tail
Of stars.

There are always a few men like me
In this world

Who are house-sitting for God.
We share His royal duties:

I water each day a favorite potted plant
Of His –
This earth.

Ask the Friend for love.
Ask Him again.

For I have learned that every heart will get
What it prays for
Most.

Just Sit There

Just sit there right now.
Don't do a thing.
Just rest.

For your separation from God
Is the hardest work in this world.

Let me bring you trays of food
And something
That you like to drink.

You can use my soft words
As a cushion
For your
Head.

A Suspended Blue Ocean

The sky
Is a suspended blue ocean.
The stars are the fish
That swim.

The planets are the white whales
I sometimes hitch a ride on,

And the sun and all light
Have forever fused themselves

Into my heart and upon
My skin.

There is only one rule
On this Wild Playground,

For every sign Hafiz has ever seen
Reads the same.

They all say,

"Have fun, my dear; my dear, have fun,
In the Beloved's Divine
Game,

O, in the Beloved's
Wonderful
Game."

A Note On Divinity

Poetry at its height is the Sun speaking. Language when it mingles with spirit does a tremendous service to the world: it empowers and changes lives; it awakens love, valor, wonder and reveals the Dance. The words of a poet-saint are unique, they become cherished friends to the heart – for they free, they constantly comfort and free.

People from many religious traditions believe that there are always living persons who are one with God. These rare souls disseminate Light upon this earth and entrust the Divine to others. Hafiz is regarded as one who came to live in that Sacred Union, and sometimes he even directly spoke of that experience in his poetry. He offered secrets, tangible keys as it were, to help those who are ready to integrate with sublime states of consciousness so they can assist in carrying out God's plan.

Someone once wrote me, "How could anyone ever say they were God?" I replied, "If God exists, if a Real God exists – one of Infinite Power – then there is Nothing that God could not do. That is, if God wanted, He could give Himself entirely to someone without ever diminishing His own state. And if you were the recipient of that Divine Gift – what would you then Know?"

Rumi, Kabir, Saadi, Shams, St. Francis and Ramakrishna are among the many known to have achieved perfection or "Union" because of their profound and intimate romance with the Beloved. They are sometimes called "Realized Souls" or "Perfect Masters." In Hafiz's own words,

> The voice of the river that has emptied into the ocean
> Now laughs and sings just like God.